IRISH CHAIN QUILTS
SINGLE, DOUBLE AND TRIPLE

Sharon Cerny Ogden

DOVER PUBLICATIONS, INC., New York

TABLE OF CONTENTS

Published in Canada by General Publishing Company, Ltd., 30 Lesmill Road, Don Mills, Toronto, Ontario.

Published in the United Kingdom by Constable and Company, Ltd., 3 The Lanchesters, 162–164 Fulham Palace Road, London W6 9ER.

Irish Chain Quilts: Single, Double and Triple, first published by Dover Publications, Inc. in 1992, is a revised and enlarged republication of *Double Irish Chain*, originally published by The Gingerbread Express, Farmingdale, New York, in 1985. Instructions and charts for the Single Irish Chain quilt and the Triple Irish Chain quilt have been added to this edition.

Manufactured in the United States of America
Dover Publications, Inc., 31 East 2nd Street, Mineola, N.Y. 11501

Library of Congress Cataloging in Publication Data

Ogden, Sharon Cerny.
    Irish chain quilts : single, double, and triple / Sharon Cerny Ogden.
        p.   cm.
    "A revised and enlarged republication of Double Irish chain, originally published by the Gingerbread Express, Farmingdale, New York, in 1985"—T.p. verso.
    ISBN 0-486-26962-0 (pbk.)
    1. Patchwork—Patterns. 2. Machine quilting—Patterns. I. Ogden, Sharon Cerny. Double Irish chain. II. Title.
TT835.037 1992
    746.9'7—dc20
                                                91-34757
                                                   CIP

INTRODUCTION

The Irish Chain quilt (whether single, double or triple) is one of the most universally known quilt patterns. The design can be traced back to Colonial days and was also popular with the Amish quiltmakers of the mid-1800s. During the 1920s–1940s, it gained even more popularity. While many quilt patterns were renamed with changes in location or with political party changes, the Irish Chain quilt kept the same name over the years.

Irish Chain designs are unusual in that they depend on two totally different blocks pieced together to form a secondary design, rather than on the traditional single block. The two blocks are sewn together alternately in rows. When the quilt is finished, it gives the appearance of having been pieced on the bias, even though all the blocks are pieced on the straight. This optical illusion contributes to the popularity of the design. Most early Irish Chains were pieced from red and white or blue and white cottons.

There are three known versions of the design—the Single Irish Chain, the Double Irish Chain and the Triple Irish Chain.

The Single Irish Chain *(Fig. 1, page 4)* consists of a nine-patch block set alternately with a plain block.

The Double Irish Chain *(Fig. 2, page 5)* is constructed of a pieced block and what is referred to as a "plain" block, even though it appears to have four smaller patches in its corners. The pieced block is made up of three fabrics arranged in a specific pattern. Rows 1 and 5 are alike, as are rows 2 and 4. Row 3 is a separate row entirely.

The Triple Irish Chain *(Fig. 3, page 6)* follows the same format as the Double Irish Chain; however, the pieced block has more patches in it and the "plain" block has three patches in each corner.

Irish Chain quilts look best when an odd number of rows, each with an odd number of blocks, is used, so that all four corners of the quilt are the same; for example, three blocks by five rows (as shown in Figs. 1–3) or five blocks by seven rows.

Traditionally, to make any of the Irish Chain variations, a square template was made and many, many small squares were cut and sewn together by hand in the traditional piecing manner. The plain blocks of the Double and Triple Irish Chains had four and twelve squares appliquéd to the corners, respectively.

This book provides a quick cutting and piecing method for Irish Chain quilts. Rather than making pattern pieces or templates, fabric is cut into strips, and the strips are sewn together on the sewing machine and then cut into rows for blocks. Even the "plain" blocks are cut in strips. Please note that this method *cannot* be used with hand-sewing since you will cut across the stitching as you sew, cut and piece the strips into blocks.

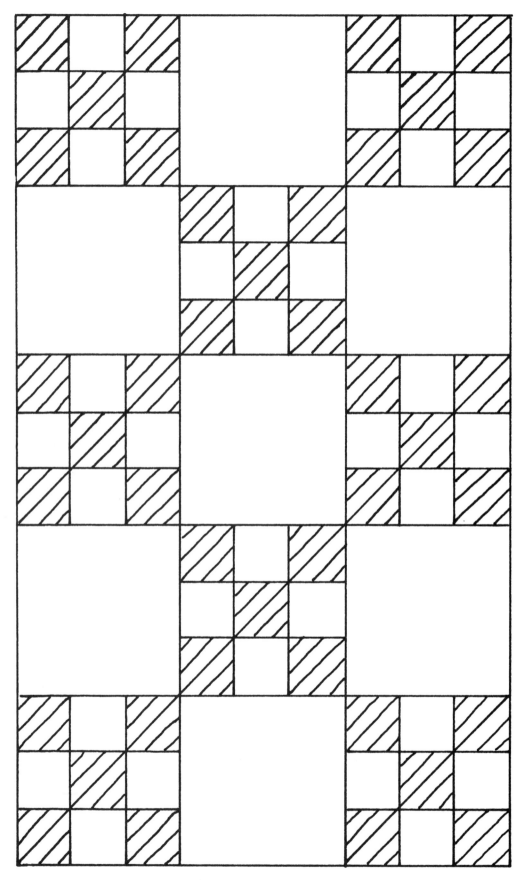

Fig. 1. Single Irish Chain Quilt

Fig. 2. Double Irish Chain Quilt

Fig. 3. Triple Irish Chain Quilt

GENERAL INSTRUCTIONS

BEFORE YOU BEGIN

To get an overall idea of the method described in this book, it is suggested that you read the book in its entirety before you begin. Consult Charts 1, 2 and 3 *(pages 16–18)* for the finished sizes of the quilts. Measure your bed with bedding on it to find the correct size to make. You can adjust the width of the borders to make slight changes in measurements, but be sure to allow extra fabric if you cut wider borders.

NOTE: When preparing the cutting charts, it was assumed that, after shrinkage, the fabric would measure approximately 41″ across the width. If your fabric is truly 45″ wide to begin with and doesn't shrink much, you will possibly get more cut rows per strip set, and therefore might have a strip set left over. But remember, it is always better to have extra fabric than not enough.

FABRICS

For the Single Irish Chain, two fabrics are used. Three fabrics are needed for the Double Irish Chain and four are used for the Triple Irish Chain.

The easiest fabrics to work with are 100% cotton calicoes. These are the traditional fabrics for quiltmaking and are still preferred by experienced quiltmakers. Cotton fabrics are cool in the summer and warm in the winter. Have you ever noticed a "mysterious" spot appear on a synthetic or blended fabric? This will not happen with cotton. With the right preparation, you will not have to worry about shrinkage in cotton. Many people complain that cotton fabrics wrinkle, but once they are sewn into your quilt and quilted, they will not

wrinkle as much as when they were first washed and dried. Cotton fabrics have been around long enough to prove they will not self-destruct at some time in the future—but synthetics haven't. If you want to use a blend, try not to use anything that has more than 30% synthetic fiber.

Choose a light and a dark fabric for the Single Irish Chain; a light, a medium and a dark for the Double Irish Chain; and a light, a medium-light, a medium and a dark for the Triple Irish Chain. The only restriction on the fabric is that the light color (or the fabric for the "plain blocks" in all three designs) should not be a solid fabric. Any of the other fabrics can be a solid fabric, but since we will be actually patching this "plain" block, we don't want the seam line to show. In the Single Irish Chain, a solid fabric *could* be used for the "plain" block since there is no seam. The fabrics can be shades of the same colors—light, medium and dark green, for example; or complementary colors—rust calico, rust print and navy pin dot, etc. *Be sure you do not pick any one-way designs.* The Double Irish Chain quilt can be made using only two colors by making the light and medium fabrics the same, and the Triple Irish Chain can be made with only three colors, either by making the medium-light and dark fabrics the same or by making the medium-light and medium fabrics the same.

BATTING

Bonded batting should be used in your Irish Chain quilt because it allows you to do a minimal amount of quilting if you wish. Choose a fluffy batt that is bonded on both sides to prevent "bearding" of the batting through the fabric. Remember, always buy a batt that is larger than your quilt top. The batting gets "taken up" as you quilt, and you wouldn't want to be short on the edges when you go to finish your quilt.

NOTIONS

Thread. Since the entire quilt top will be machine-pieced, sew it with a neutral shade of cotton-covered polyester thread. White (available in the larger dressmakers' spools) is recommended unless you are working primarily with darker colors. Since all seams will be pressed to one side, the seam stitching will not be visible. You will save time by winding two to three bobbins of thread before you start. That way you won't have to stop to rewind bobbins when you run out; you can just pop in a filled one.

Strip-Cutting Boards. These boards are made to simplify marking strips of fabric. They are about 24″ long and come in a variety of widths. They can be made out of any sturdy material, but are generally Plexiglas or Masonite. The Masonite ones tend to work best because they do not slip on the fabric. They are a great tool for borders, too. Strip boards can be carefully placed side by side to create wider strips—for instance, a 3½″-wide board + a 4½″-wide board = an 8″-wide board. You will need the following widths for your quilt:

SINGLE IRISH CHAIN
2½″ (all sizes except king)
3½″ (king)
4½″ (all sizes)
6½″ (twin)

DOUBLE IRISH CHAIN
1½″ (double)
2½″ (all sizes)
3½″ (double, queen & king)
4½″ (baby & twin)
5½″ (king)
6½″ (all sizes)

TRIPLE IRISH CHAIN
2″ (all sizes)
3½″ (baby, twin & double)
4½″ (queen & king)
5″ (all sizes)
5½″ (double)
6½″ (queen & king)
8″ (all sizes)

Do not tear your strips, since tearing tends to distort the fabric. You will be sewing ¼″-wide seams on the sewing machine and it is sometimes difficult to determine the precise edge of a torn strip because of fraying.

Marking tools. A #2 soft lead pencil is good for marking most fabrics; use a white marking pencil if using dark fabrics.

A right triangle or a T-square (Fig. 4). These are needed for squaring off the fabric before marking. A right triangle can be made out of sturdy template plastic and can be used for many other quilt projects. It is a handy tool to have.

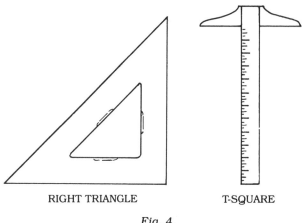

RIGHT TRIANGLE   T-SQUARE

Fig. 4.

Cutting tools. You will need sharp scissors or a rotary cutter and mat. I prefer to work with scissors.

Pins. Pins will not be necessary until you are ready to put the three layers of your quilt together for basting and quilting. At that time, you should use extra-long glass-head pins made especially for quilters.

Quilting needles and quilting thread. Quilting needles are called "betweens," and come in sizes 7 to 10. The larger the number, the smaller the needle. Use the smallest needle you are comfortable with. You may want to wait until your quilt top is finished before you decide what color thread to use for quilting—it depends upon the effect you want to create and how much quilting you want to do. Choose a thread color that either blends with or contrasts with the "plain" block fabric, since that is the block that will contain the most quilting.

FABRIC PREPARATION

Yardage amounts are given in the cutting charts for each quilt (see Charts 1, 2 and 3, pages 16–18). Be sure to wash and dry all fabrics before marking and cutting. This is very important for two reasons. First, you want to pre-shrink the fabrics. Second, you want to be sure that the fabrics are colorfast. Fabrics that continue to bleed after they have been soaked should be used with caution and possibly eliminated.

You can soak your fabric in a bowl of hot water from the tap, then wring it dry and put in your dryer or line-dry it. Do not use fabric softeners or fabric softener sheets in your dryer—they will make the fabric limp. If you have a large amount of the same fabric, you may want to put it in the last rinse cycle of your washing machine, rinse it, spin it dry and then finish drying it in your dryer or on the line. Press any wrinkled fabric at this point.

Before you are ready to mark your fabric, you will have to straighten it. All fabric must be straightened; it does not matter who the manufacturer is or how much you paid for the fabric. Hold the fabric (about 24″ of it) inside out with the selvages together. Hold it up so that it hangs free and does not rest on a table. Check for a telltale wrinkle across the bottom of the fabric. If this wrinkle appears, slightly adjust the fabric, shifting the selvages back and forth as necessary until the fabric hangs straight. Once you have accomplished this, carefully lay the fabric down on your worktable. On some fabrics, you may notice a difference of 3″ to 4″. Line up your right triangle or T-square at the *fold* of the fabric and draw a line that is exactly perpendicular to the fold *(Fig. 5)*. Extend that line

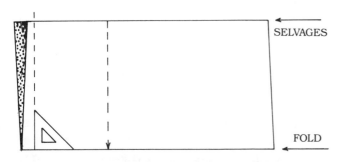

SELVAGES

FOLD

Fig. 5. Draw a line perpendicular to the fold.

with a strip-cutting board across the width of the folded fabric and you are ready to start. All fabric is cut across the fold with the crosswise grain. Cut strips must be exactly perpendicular to the fold, otherwise they will not be straight when you open the fabric.

MARKING AND CUTTING THE STRIPS

The following directions are for drawing and cutting with a pair of scissors. If you feel you are proficient with a rotary cutter, please feel free to use one; however, be aware that accuracy is imperative. If you discover an error in your strips as you are drawing lines on the back of your fabric, you can always correct it by redrawing the lines. If you use a rotary cutter, correcting an error is not so simple, and you can waste both time and fabric having to recut.

Marking and cutting the fabric are two of the most important steps in quilting. You must be accurate in order to have the blocks fit together correctly. You can now proceed to draw and cut the number of strips indicated on the cutting chart for each quilt.

Mark all the lines first and then cut for each fabric. Always mark your strips on the wrong side of the fabric. This way, if there is an error and you discover it prior to cutting, it can be corrected without ruining your fabric. Check for the "squareness" of your lines every five to six strips. An easy way to count your strips is to number each fifth strip. Mark the appropriate number of strips following Chart 1, 2 or 3 on pages 16–18 *(Fig. 6)*.

It is best to mark and cut all of the strips for the blocks first, then cut any necessary strips for your borders.

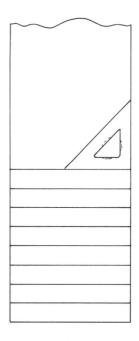

Fig. 6. Mark the appropriate number of strips on the wrong side of the fabric.

SEWING THE STRIPS

You will be sewing the strips together following Chart 4 for Single Irish Chain (*page 19*), Chart 5 for Double Irish Chain (*page 19*) or Chart 6 for Triple Irish Chain (*page 20*). These sewing charts show you the arrangement of the fabric and what the finished strip set should look like, how many of each strip set to make and how many rows to cut from each strip set for each size quilt.

Sew all strips with a ¼″ seam allowance. The presser foot on most sewing machines is ¼″ wide. If your presser foot is not ¼″ wide (measuring from the needle to the outer edge), place a piece of masking tape on the base of your machine to indicate the ¼″ mark. Set your machine for 8–12 stitches per inch.

You will be sewing all your fabrics using "mass-production" sewing techniques. There is no need to pin the fabrics before sewing them because you will be sewing straight edges. Simply match up the edges of the strips, line up the presser foot with the edge of the fabric and sew away. Do not force the fabric through the machine; let the machine do the work. Instead of cutting the thread at the end of each strip, have the next strip ready to be sewn and feed it right into the machine (*Fig. 7*). This saves not only time but money, too, because you will be using less thread. After all the strips are sewn, clip them apart.

WRONG SIDE
OF FABRIC

Fig. 7. Sewing the strips together with "mass-production" sewing techniques.

You will always sew your strips in the correct order if you remember that you always put the fabric that is to the left in Charts 4, 5 or 6 against the base of the machine facing right side up and the fabric to the right of it in the chart facing down on top of the first fabric. Strips should be sewn together in pairs. The pairs are then sewn together and the extra strip added to the group. Sew all the strips for one row before continuing to another row.

After all your strips are sewn, you are ready to press them. Press the seams to one side (preferably toward the darker of the fabrics). *Do not press the seams open.* Do not stretch and pull the fabric as you are pressing and be sure that you are not pressing your strips into "rainbows"—if this occurs, dampen the fabric and try again. You may also want to press the fabrics on the right side after you have pressed the seams to one side on the wrong side.

MARKING AND CUTTING ROW SETS

You are now ready to mark and cut your sewn strips into rows using the appropriate strip-cutting board (*Fig. 8*):

> Single Irish Chain—use a 4½″-wide strip board
> Double Irish Chain—use a 2½″-wide strip board
> Triple Irish Chain—use a 2″-wide strip board

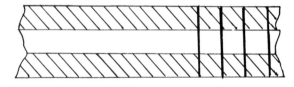

Fig. 8. Marking the rows.

NOTE: Cut *only* the number of rows indicated by the last column in Chart 4, 5 or 6. Mark all lines on the wrong side of the fabric first and then cut. As you can see, you have now completed the "rows" for your pieced blocks.

PIECING THE BLOCKS

Now you are ready to piece your blocks. If you have been accurate in your marking, piecing and cutting, you can just lay the correct rows on top of each other without pinning. If you feel more secure pinning the blocks to match up the corners, please feel free to do so.

Single Irish Chain
Sew half of your Row 1 strips to all of the Row 2 strips, using mass-production sewing techniques *(Fig. 9)*. Do not cut the units apart.

Sew the remaining Row 1 strips to the Row 2 side of these Row 1/Row 2 groups to create the nine-patch blocks *(Fig. 10)*.

Cut the blocks apart by snipping the continuous threads between the blocks. Press the blocks.

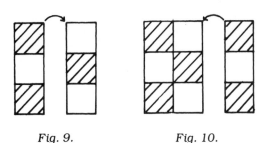

Fig. 9.   Fig. 10.

Double Irish Chain
Sew all of your Row 1 strips to your Row 2 strips *(Fig. 11)*. Sew your Row 3 strips between two sets of Row 1/Row 2 strips so that they are in the following order: Row 1, Row 2, Row 3, Row 2, Row 1 *(Fig. 12)*.

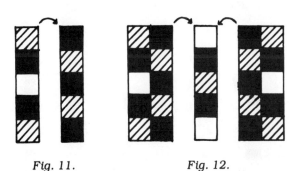

Fig. 11.   Fig. 12.

Triple Irish Chain
Sew all Row 1 strips to Row 2 strips *(Fig. 13)*. Sew *half* of the Row 3 strips to Row 4 strips *(Fig. 14)*. Sew the remaining Row 3 strips to the Row 4 side of these units so you have Row 3/Row 4/Row 3 groups *(Fig. 15)*.

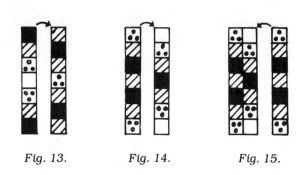

Fig. 13.   Fig. 14.   Fig. 15.

Sew half of the Row 1/Row 2 groups to the Row 3/Row 4/Row 3 groups *(Fig. 16)*. Sew the remaining Row 1/Row 2 groups to the Row 3 side of these units *(Fig. 17)*.

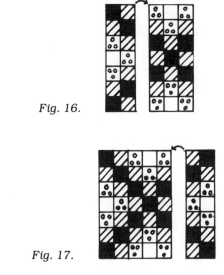

Fig. 16.

Fig. 17.

PLAIN BLOCKS

After you have completed all the pieced blocks, you will be ready to piece the "plain" blocks. NOTE: Continue to use "mass-production" sewing techniques—do not break the threads between sewing rows together; just feed the next two rows into the machine and keep going.

Single Irish Chain
These blocks are already cut and ready to use. They truly are "plain" blocks and no piecing is necessary.

Double Irish Chain
To sew the "plain" blocks, count out half of the cut "plain" strips (wide light fabric and narrow dark fabric combination).

Place a 6½"-wide light strip of fabric right side up on the sewing machine, and sew the cut "plain" strips to the long side of this strip with a ¼" seam allowance (Fig. 18).

Butt the strips together and continue sewing until half the "plain" strips are used up. Then carefully mark and cut strips apart (Fig. 19) and sew the remaining cut "plain" strips to the opposite side of the 6½"-wide strip. You have now completed all the "plain" blocks (Fig. 20).

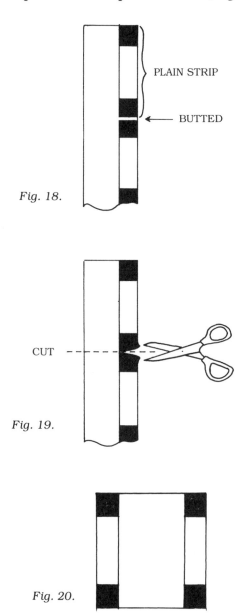

Fig. 18.

Fig. 19.

Fig. 20.

Triple Irish Chain

The process is similar to the Double Irish Chain; however, you must first sew together the Row A/Row B combinations. Sew all Row A and Row B strips together (Fig. 21). Count out half of these combination strips. Sew these strips to

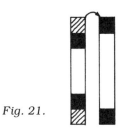

Fig. 21.

the remaining 5"-wide light strips, sewing the Row B side of the combination A/B rows to the long side of the 5"-wide strips. Carefully mark and cut the strips apart (Fig. 22). Sew the remaining A/B combination rows to the opposite side (again, the B row is next to the light fabric) (Fig. 23). You have now completed the "plain" block (Fig. 24).

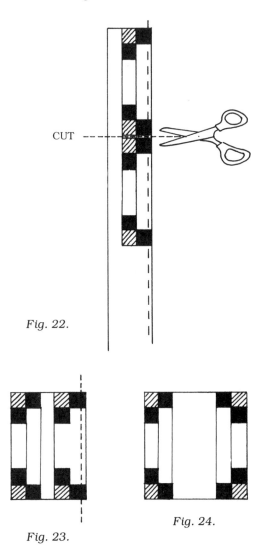

Fig. 22.

Fig. 23.

Fig. 24.

PIECING THE QUILT TOP

Press all pieced and "plain" blocks on both the wrong and right sides. You are now ready to piece your quilt top. Row 1 will be pieced as follows: pieced block, plain block, pieced block, etc. (the exact number depends on the size of your quilt), ending the row with a pieced block. Row 2 starts and ends with a plain block. For the correct number of rows to sew together, consult Chart 1 for the Single Irish Chain, Chart 2 for the Double Irish Chain and Chart 3 for the Triple Irish Chain. Your last row should be identical to your first row (Fig. 25).

Press the quilt top.

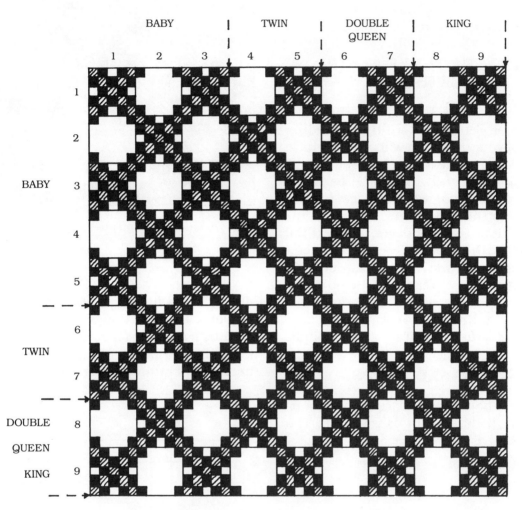

Fig. 25. Layout for Double Irish Chain.

BORDERS

You are now ready to put the finishing touch on your quilt top with the borders. The light (or medium-light) and dark colors are used for the borders. The light color is added first. Sew the top and bottom borders to the quilt, then sew on the side borders. When the light border is complete, sew on the dark border in the same manner. Depending on the size of the quilt, the border strips may have to be pieced before sewing them to the quilt top.

QUILTING DESIGNS

A quilt is made up of three layers—a top (machine-pieced in this case), a lining or batting, and a backing (usually plain). In order to keep the three layers from shifting, they must be joined in some way. To do this, quilts can be tied at intervals or, more commonly, stitched through all three layers. Both the stitches and the process of making them are called "quilting."

Several quilt designs suitable for the plain

blocks (shamrock, house, apple, hearts, a basket, etc.) are given on pages 21–30. You can make a template from plastic and trace the design onto the middle of the plain block with a #2 pencil, or you can transfer the design using a light box. If you do not have a light box, you can tape the design to a window and hold the quilt over it. You should now be able to see through the fabric to trace the design.

PUTTING THE THREE LAYERS TOGETHER

Your backing should be 3″ to 4″ larger than your quilt top in both length and width. Depending on the size of your quilt, you will probably have to join lengths of fabric for the backing.

To assemble the quilt, place the backing, wrong side up, on your work surface. Spread the batting over the backing and smooth it out; center the quilt top, right side up, on top of the batting. Pin the three layers together with long quilter's pins. With white thread, baste every 6″ both horizontally and vertically. Remove the pins and you are ready to quilt. Beware of basting with colored thread. It can leave small dots of dye on your quilt where it is sewn through.

FRAMES AND HOOPS

Often a piece to be quilted is placed in a frame or hoop to keep the layers taut as you work. The choice is yours as to whether or not to use a frame or a hoop.

A full-size frame is nice to use if you have the room. A quilting hoop resembles a large embroidery hoop.

QUILTING

The quilting stitch is a simple running stitch worked through all three layers. Your stitches should all be equal in length and should be the same length on the front and the back of your quilt. It is easiest to quilt toward your body. Your thread should be no longer than 18″ to reduce twisting and knotting as you work.

Starting in the center, quilt the plain blocks as desired. Also quilt ¼″ from the edge of the plain blocks (Fig. 26).

Quilting is not strictly necessary in the pieced blocks, but if you wish, quilt ¼″ in from the edge of either all the dark squares or all the

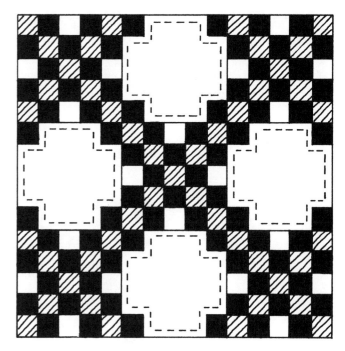

Fig. 26. Quilt ¼″ in from the edge of the "plain" blocks.

medium and light squares for the best effect. Or you can quilt diagonally through all the medium colors—forming continuous lines (Fig. 27). You can basically use your own imagination and quilt however you want.

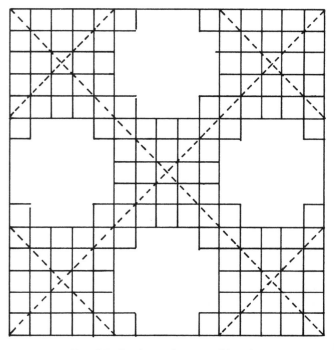

Fig. 27. Quilting the pieced blocks.

FINISHING THE EDGE OF THE QUILT

After all the quilting is finished, trim the top, batt and backing evenly. Fold the back of the quilt in ¼″ over the batting; fold the top under ¼″ to meet the edge of the back. Pin carefully. Join by quilting ⅛″ or less from the edge. This will create a knife edge on the quilt.

SIGNING AND DATING YOUR QUILT

As a quilt historian, I cannot stress enough the importance of signing and dating your work, just as an artist signs and dates his work. Try to include the town and state as well. This can be incorporated into your quilt or stitched onto a separate fabric that is then attached to your quilt.

CHART 1: Cutting Chart for Single Irish Chain

Size	Color	Yardage Required	Cut for Blocks	Cut for Borders
Baby 40" × 64" 15 blocks 3 blocks × 5 blocks 8 pieced & 7 plain	Light Dark Back	1⅝ yd. 1 yd. 2 yds.	4—4½"-wide strips; 7—12½" squares 5—4½"-wide strips —	None 5—2½" wide strips —
Twin 76" × 100" 35 blocks 5 blocks × 7 blocks 18 pieced & 17 plain	Light Dark Back	4 yds. 3 yds. 6 yds.	8—4½"-wide strips; 17—12½" squares 10—4½"-wide strips —	9—2½"-wide strips 9—6½"-wide strips —
Double 88" × 116" 63 blocks 7 blocks × 9 blocks 32 pieced & 31 plain	Light Dark Back	6 yds. 3⅜ yds. 7½ yds.	16—4½"-wide strips; 31—12½" squares 20—4½"-wide strips —	None 10—2½"-wide strips —
Queen 96" × 120" 63 blocks 7 blocks × 9 blocks 32 pieced & 31 plain	Light Dark Back	6¾ yds. 4 yds. 8⅓ yds.	16—4½"-wide strips; 31—12½" squares 20—4½"-wide strips —	11—2½"-wide strips 11—4½"-wide strips —
King 114" × 114" 81 blocks 9 blocks × 9 blocks 41 pieced & 40 plain	Light Dark Back	7½ yds. 4½ yds. 9½ yds.	20—4½"-wide strips; 40—12½" squares 25—4½"-wide strips —	None 12—3½" strips —

CHART 2: Cutting Chart for Double Irish Chain

Size	Color	Yardage Required	Cut for Blocks	Cut for Borders
Baby 42" × 62" 15 blocks 3 blocks × 5 blocks 8 pieced & 7 plain	Light Medium Dark Back	1⅛ yds. ⅜ yd. 1½ yds. 2 yds.	3—2½"-wide strips; 4—6½"-wide strips 5—2½"-wide strips 9—2½"-wide strips —	4—2½"-wide strips None 5—4½" wide strips —
Twin 62" × 102" 45 blocks 5 blocks × 9 blocks 23 pieced & 22 plain	Light Medium Dark Back	2¾ yds. 1⅛ yds. 3⅓ yds. 6 yds.	7—2½"-wide strips; 9—6½"-wide strips 14—2½"-wide strips 25—2½"-wide strips —	7—2½"-wide strips None 8—4½"-wide strips —
Double 78" × 98" 63 blocks 7 blocks × 9 blocks 32 pieced & 31 plain	Light Medium Dark Back	3⅜ yds. 1½ yds. 3½ yds. 6 yds.	8—2½"-wide strips; 12—6½"-wide strips 18—2½"-wide strips 32—2½"-wide strips —	8—1½"-wide strips None 9—3½"-wide strips —
Queen 88" × 108" 63 blocks 7 blocks × 9 blocks 32 pieced & 31 plain	Light Medium Dark Back	3¾ yds. 1½ yds. 4¼ yds. 7½ yds.	8—2½"-wide strips; 12—6½"-wide strips 18—2½"-wide strips 32—2½"-wide strips —	8—3½"-wide strips None 10—6½"-wide strips —
King 106" × 106" 81 blocks 9 blocks × 9 blocks 41 pieced & 40 plain	Light Medium Dark Back	4¾ yds. 2⅛ yds. 5 yds. 9 yds.	14—2½"-wide strips; 16—6½"-wide strips 28—2½"-wide strips 48—2½"-wide strips —	9—3½"-wide strips None 10—5½"-wide strips —

CHART 3: Cutting Chart for Triple Irish Chain

Size	Color	Yardage Required	Cut for Blocks	Cut for Borders
Baby 37½" × 58½" 15 blocks 3 blocks × 5 blocks 8 pieced & 7 plain	Light	1¼ yds.	3—2"-wide strips; 4—5"-wide strips; 1—8"-wide strip	None
	Med. Lt.	½ yd.	7—2"-wide strips	None
	Medium	⅞ yd.	13—2"-wide strips	None
	Dark	1¼ yds.	11—2"-wide strips	5—3½"-wide strips
	Back	2 yds.	—	—
Twin 68½" × 89½" 35 blocks 5 blocks × 7 blocks 18 pieced & 17 plain	Light	1⅞ yds.	4—2"-wide strips; 8—5"-wide strips; 2—8"-wide strips	None
	Med. Lt.	1½ yds.	12—2"-wide strips	8—3½"-wide strips
	Medium	1½ yds.	26—2"-wide strips	None
	Dark	2⅝ yds.	21—2"-wide strips	9—5½"-wide strips
	Back	5¼ yds.	—	—
Double 89½" × 110½" 63 blocks 7 blocks × 9 blocks 32 pieced & 31 plain	Light	3½ yds.	8—2"-wide strips; 15—5"-wide strips; 4—8"-wide strips	None
	Med. Lt.	2¼ yds.	24—2"-wide strips	9—3½"-wide strips
	Medium	2¾ yds.	48—2"-wide strips	None
	Dark	4 yds.	42—2"-wide strips	10—5½"-wide strips
	Back	7½ yds.	—	—
Queen 93½" × 114½" 63 blocks 7 blocks × 9 blocks 32 pieced & 31 plain	Light	3½ yds.	8—2"-wide strips; 15—5"-wide strips; 4—8"-wide strips	None
	Med. Lt.	2⅝ yds.	24—2"-wide strips	10—4½"-wide strips
	Medium	2¾ yds.	48—2"-wide strips	None
	Dark	4½ yds.	42—2"-wide strips	11—6½"-wide strips
	Back	8½ yds.	—	—
King 114½" × 114½" 81 blocks 9 blocks × 9 blocks 41 pieced & 40 plain	Light	4¼ yds.	11—2"-wide strips; 18—5"-wide strips; 4—8"-wide strips	None
	Med. Lt.	3½ yds.	31—2"-wide strips	11—4½"-wide strips
	Medium	3⅜ yds.	59—2"-wide strips	None
	Dark	5 yds.	49—2"-wide strips	12—6½"-wide strips
	Back	10 yds.	—	—

CHART 4: Sewing Chart for Single Irish Chain

Sewn Strip		Size	# of Pieced Blocks	# of Sewn Strip Sets	# of 4½"-wide Cut Rows
Row 1	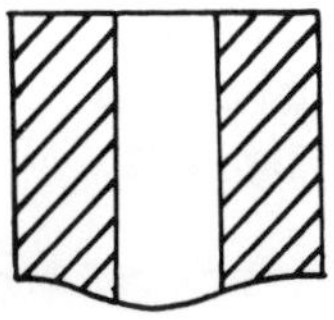	Baby	8	2	16
		Twin	18	4	36
		Double	32	8	64
		Queen	32	8	64
		King	41	10	82
Row 2	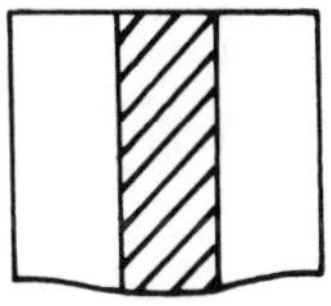	Baby	8	1	8
		Twin	18	2	18
		Double	32	4	32
		Queen	32	4	32
		King	41	5	41

▢ LIGHT   ▨ DARK

CHART 5: Sewing Chart for Double Irish Chain

Sewn Strip		Size	# of Pieced Blocks	# of Sewn Strip Sets	# of 2½"-wide Cut Rows
Row 1		Baby	8	1	16
		Twin	23	3	46
		Double	32	4	64
		Queen	32	4	64
		King	41	6	82
Row 2		Baby	8	1	16
		Twin	23	3	46
		Double	32	4	64
		Queen	32	4	64
		King	41	6	82
Row 3		Baby	8	1	8
		Twin	23	2	23
		Double	32	2	32
		Queen	32	2	32
		King	41	3	41

Sewn Strip		Size	# of "Plain" Blocks	# of Sewn Strip Sets	# of 2½"-wide Cut Rows
"Plain" strip		Baby	7	1	14
		Twin	22	3	44
		Double	31	4	62
		Queen	31	4	62
		King	40	5	80

▢ LIGHT   ▨ MEDIUM   ■ DARK

CHART 6: Sewing Chart for Triple Irish Chain

Sewn Strip		Size	# of Pieced Blocks	# of Sewn Strip Sets	# of 2"-wide Cut Rows
Row 1	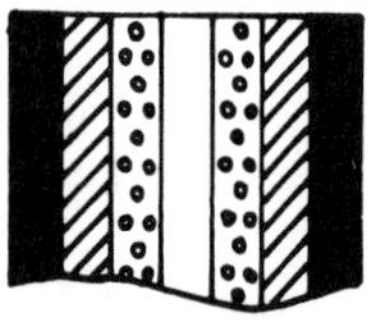	Baby	8	1	16
		Twin	18	2	36
		Double	32	4	64
		Queen	32	4	64
		King	41	5	82
Row 2	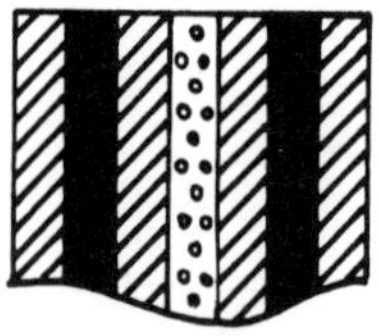	Baby	8	1	16
		Twin	18	2	36
		Double	32	4	64
		Queen	32	4	64
		King	41	5	82
Row 3		Baby	8	1	16
		Twin	18	2	36
		Double	32	4	64
		Queen	32	4	64
		King	41	5	82
Row 4		Baby	8	1	8
		Twin	18	1	18
		Double	32	2	32
		Queen	32	2	32
		King	41	3	41

Sewn Strip		Size	# of "Plain" Blocks	# of Sewn Strip Sets	# of 2"-wide Cut Rows
"Plain" Block Row A		Baby	7	1	14
		Twin	17	2	34
		Double	31	4	62
		Queen	31	4	62
		King	40	4	80
"Plain" Block Row B	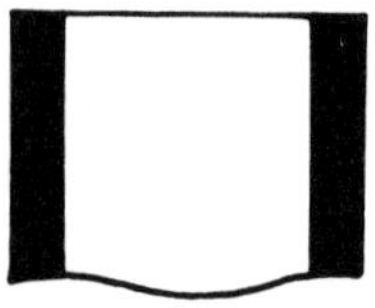	Baby	7	1	14
		Twin	17	2	34
		Double	31	4	62
		Queen	31	4	62
		King	40	4	80

□ LIGHT   ⊡ MED. LT.   ▨ MEDIUM   ■ DARK

24

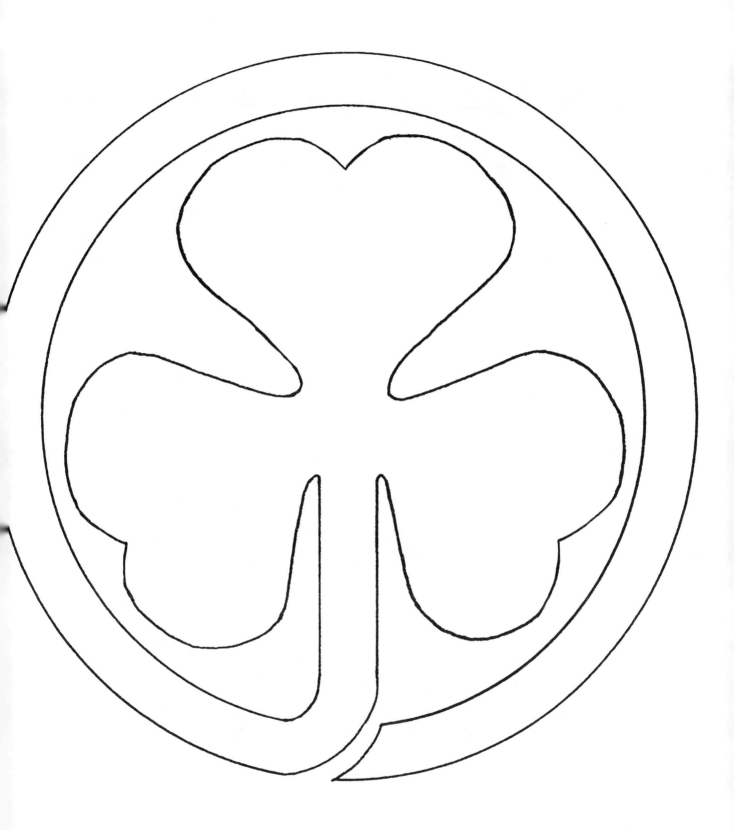

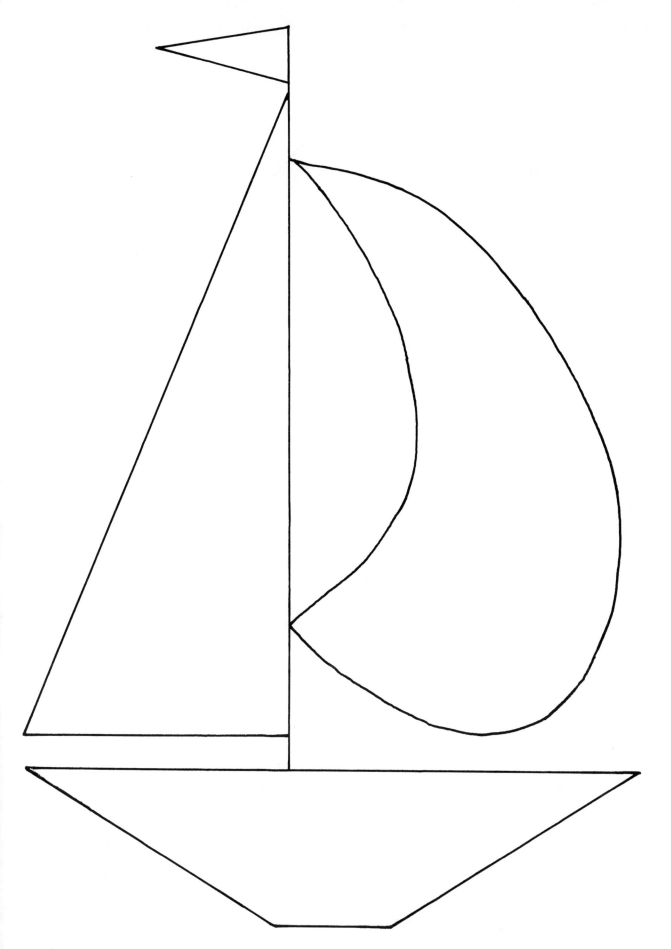

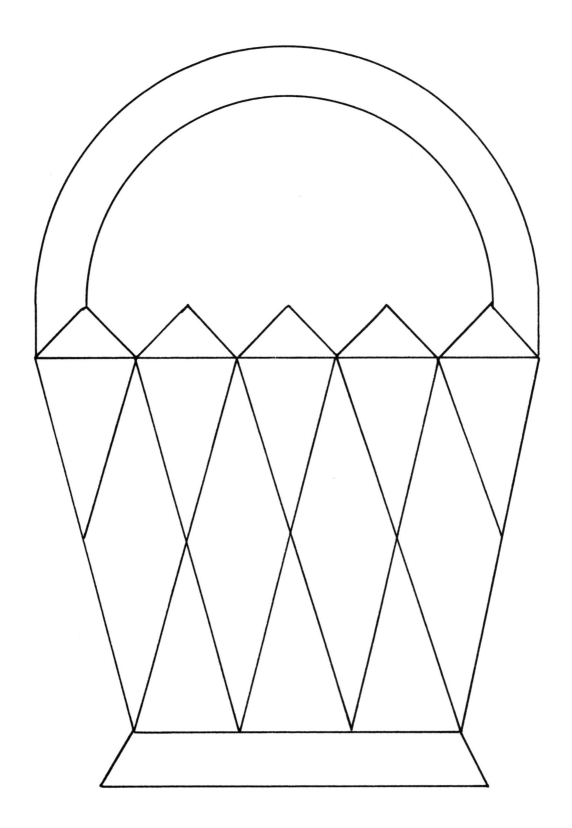

METRIC CONVERSION CHART

CONVERTING INCHES TO CENTIMETERS AND YARDS TO METERS

mm — millimeters   cm — centimeters   m — meters

INCHES INTO MILLIMETERS AND CENTIMETERS
(Slightly rounded off for convenience)

inches	mm		cm	inches	cm	inches	cm	inches	cm
1/8	3mm			5	12.5	21	53.5	38	96.5
1/4	6mm			5½	14	22	56	39	99
3/8	10mm	or	1cm	6	15	23	58.5	40	101.5
1/2	13mm	or	1.3cm	7	18	24	61	41	104
5/8	15mm	or	1.5cm	8	20.5	25	63.5	42	106.5
3/4	20mm	or	2cm	9	23	26	66	43	109
7/8	22mm	or	2.2cm	10	25.5	27	68.5	44	112
1	25mm	or	2.5cm	11	28	28	71	45	114.5
1¼	32mm	or	3.2cm	12	30.5	29	73.5	46	117
1½	38mm	or	3.8cm	13	33	30	76	47	119.5
1¾	45mm	or	4.5cm	14	35.5	31	79	48	122
2	50mm	or	5cm	15	38	32	81.5	49	124.5
2½	65mm	or	6.5cm	16	40.5	33	84	50	127
3	75mm	or	7.5cm	17	43	34	86.5		
3½	90mm	or	9cm	18	46	35	89		
4	100mm	or	10cm	19	48.5	36	91.5		
4½	115mm	or	11.5cm	20	51	37	94		

YARDS TO METERS
(Slightly rounded off for convenience)

yards	meters	yards	meters	yards	meters	yards	meters	yards	meters
1/8	0.15	2⅛	1.95	4⅛	3.80	6⅛	5.60	8⅛	7.45
1/4	0.25	2¼	2.10	4¼	3.90	6¼	5.75	8¼	7.55
3/8	0.35	2⅜	2.20	4⅜	4.00	6⅜	5.85	8⅜	7.70
1/2	0.50	2½	2.30	4½	4.15	6½	5.95	8½	7.80
5/8	0.60	2⅝	2.40	4⅝	4.25	6⅝	6.10	8⅝	7.90
3/4	0.70	2¾	2.55	4¾	4.35	6¾	6.20	8¾	8.00
7/8	0.80	2⅞	2.65	4⅞	4.50	6⅞	6.30	8⅞	8.15
1	0.95	3	2.75	5	4.60	7	6.40	9	8.25
1⅛	1.05	3⅛	2.90	5⅛	4.70	7⅛	6.55	9⅛	8.35
1¼	1.15	3¼	3.00	5¼	4.80	7¼	6.65	9¼	8.50
1⅜	1.30	3⅜	3.10	5⅜	4.95	7⅜	6.75	9⅜	8.60
1½	1.40	3½	3.20	5½	5.05	7½	6.90	9½	8.70
1⅝	1.50	3⅝	3.35	5⅝	5.15	7⅝	7.00	9⅝	8.80
1¾	1.60	3¾	3.45	5¾	5.30	7¾	7.10	9¾	8.95
1⅞	1.75	3⅞	3.55	5⅞	5.40	7⅞	7.20	9⅞	9.05
2	1.85	4	3.70	6	5.50	8	7.35	10	9.15

AVAILABLE FABRIC WIDTHS

25"	65cm	50"	127cm
27"	70cm	54"/56"	140cm
35"/36"	90cm	58"/60"	150cm
39"	100cm	68"/70"	175cm
44"/45"	115cm	72"	180cm
48"	122cm		

AVAILABLE ZIPPER LENGTHS

4"	10cm	10"	25cm	22"	55cm
5"	12cm	12"	30cm	24"	60cm
6"	15cm	14"	35cm	26"	65cm
7"	18cm	16"	40cm	28"	70cm
8"	20cm	18"	45cm	30"	75cm
9"	22cm	20"	50cm		

ABOUT THE AUTHOR

Sharon Cerny Ogden, quilt teacher and historian, is noted for her quick piecing and sewing methods. A quilter for over 15 years, she has published articles in *The Professional Quilter* magazine on quilt retailing and teaching, and in *The Chronicle* of the Early American Industries Association on quilt history and she is the editor of the *Long Island Antique Bottle Association Newsletter*. Sharon also owned and operated a quilt shop, The Gingerbread House, in Farmingdale, NY, for five years. In 1986, she was nominated "Quilt Teacher of the Year" by *The Professional Quilter* magazine. In September 1986, she was chosen "Retailer of the Month" by *Craft and Needlework News* and in the Spring of 1988, she received the "Distinguished Leadership Award for the Preservation of Quilting in America" from the Biographical Institute of America.

More recently, Sharon has pursued her career in quilting along a different path. Dressed in authentically detailed reproduction clothing, using her quilts she tells the story of the life of a woman in the 1850s and the hardships she might face. Along with her husband Oliver, she travels throughout America, performing this presentation for historical organizations and at Living History Museums such as Landis Valley Farm Museum in Lancaster, Pennsylvania, Old Economy Village in Ambridge, Pennsylvania, New Harmony Historical Site in New Harmony, Indiana and Scott-Fanton Museum in Danbury, Connecticut.